Michele Kahney

"This is a refreshingly accessible treatment of a serious subject, the means and mysteries of improving education in our schools. Murphy's long-term engagement with research and practice in school improvement shines through in his willingness to grapple with the dilemmas that confront the best-intentioned efforts to bring about change in schools. The book affords us with insights drawn from the experience of one of America's leading education scholars of the past several decades."
—Philip Hallinger, Joseph Lau Professor of
Leadership and Change
Hong Kong Institute of Education

"Indicting, elucidating, and inspiring. Wrapped in an engaging, satirical, CSI-like investigation of the death and reincarnation (again!) of Mr. School Improvement, Murphy's proverbs ring true to the best of our knowledge from decades of research and toil in the school improvement vineyard. This book will challenge and guide those who take school improvement seriously—teachers, principals, superintendents, designers and consultants, captains of the school improvement industry, civic leaders, policy makers, and researchers alike. I will keep this volume within short reach and refer to it often. I strongly recommend it to all who aspire to better understand, lead, and succeed at this most important work."
—Mark A. Smylie, Professor of Education
University of Illinois at Chicago

This book is dedicated to colleagues whose labors

in the school improvement vineyard

unlocked these lessons for me.

JOSEPH MURPHY

THE ARCHITECTURE
of School Improvement

LESSONS LEARNED

CORWIN
A SAGE Company

CORWIN
A SAGE Company

FOR INFORMATION:

Corwin
A SAGE Company
2455 Teller Road
Thousand Oaks, California 91320
www.corwin.com

SAGE Ltd.
1 Oliver's Yard
55 City Road
London EC1Y 1SP
United Kingdom

SAGE India Pvt. Ltd.
B 1/I 1 Mohan Cooperative Industrial Area
Mathura Road, New Delhi 110 044
India

SAGE Publications Asia-Pacific Pte. Ltd.
3 Church Street
#10-04 Samsung Hub
Singapore 049483

Acquisitions Editor: Arnis Burvikovs
Associate Editor: Desirée A. Bartlett
Editorial Assistant: Mayan White
Permissions Editor: Jennifer Barron
Project Editor: Veronica Stapleton
Copy Editor: Laurie Pitman
Typesetter: Hurix Systems Pvt. Ltd.
Proofreader: Scott Oney
Indexer: Sheila Bodell
Cover Designer: Rose Storey

Printed in the United States of America

Library of Congress Cataloging-in-Publication Data

Murphy, Joseph, 1949-
The architecture of school improvement: lessons learned / Joseph Murphy.

pages cm

Includes bibliographical references and index.

ISBN 978-1-4522-6822-4 (pbk.)

1. School improvement programs—United States. I. Title.

LB2822.82.M87 2013

371.2'07—dc23

2013005349

This book is printed on acid-free paper.

Certified Chain of Custody
SUSTAINABLE FORESTRY INITIATIVE
Promoting Sustainable Forestry
www.sfiprogram.org
SFI-01268

SFI label applies to text stock

13 14 15 16 17 10 9 8 7 6 5 4 3 2 1

Contents

The DNA of School Improvement   vii

Preface   ix

About the Author   xi

Tales of School Improvement   1

The Mournful Tale of the Death of
Mr. School Improvement   2

The Case of the Remarkable Reappearance
of Mr. School Improvement   11

The Return of Mr. School Improvement   19

Framework for School Improvement   27

Essential Lessons   33

Epilogue   115

References   117

Index   119

The DNA of School Improvement

Common Wisdom of School Improvement

Set and Pursue Challenging Targets of Performance
For Everyone

Hire and Retain Good People

Provide Everyone with the Tools They Need to do Their Work

Create Coherence; Get All the Pieces of the System Aligned

Pay Attention to Your Customers

Hold Everyone Accountable for the Quality of
Their Performance

The Enemies of School Improvement

Helplessness

Denial

Complacency

Blame

Distrust

Isolation

Fragmentation

Overload

Preface

This volume follows a quite straightforward design. On each page, I label, then explain an "essential lesson" of school improvement, lessons that I have been accumulating for the past 35 years. These lessons are intended to take us into the part of the school improvement story line that is least developed. The more well-developed part of the narrative is concerned with the "content" of school improvement (e.g., quality instruction, leadership). The content can be thought of as the building material of school improvement. The essential lessons are best thought of as the rules of school improvement construction (e.g., in building, we need to attend to both academic press and school culture; neither one alone is sufficient). We can also think of them as "guiding principles."

I attempt to deepen the story line on essential lessons in a unique, and I hope engaging and explanatory manner. Specifically, I illustrate these lessons in three "tales" of school reform, all centered on the death and return of Mr. School Improvement and the work of three forensic school improvement detectives—Mr. Wolf, C.B., and Barnabus Dolphin. The tales are a bit of a blend of the work of A. A. Milne and Kenneth Grahame and their leading actors and Arthur Conan Doyle and his gifted protagonist Sherlock Holmes. Each tale is scaffolded on the essential lessons described in the book but in a way that allows the reader to discover them for himself or herself. One can also return to the tales and see the lessons clearly once they are presented in a more direct manner.

Depending on your point of view, you will find the characters in the tales odd or cute or endearing. My intent and my hope is that you will fall on the right-hand side of the interpretative continuum. Wherever you land on that assessment, because good schools are always a combination of the right content and the right guiding principles, I believe that you will find these lessons to be of real assistance in the work of building schools in which all youngsters are truly successful.

About the Author

Joseph Murphy is the Frank W. Mayborn Chair and associate dean at Vanderbilt's Peabody College of Education. He has also been a faculty member at the University of Illinois and The Ohio State University, where he was the William Ray Flesher Professor of Education.

In the public schools, he has served as an administrator at the school, district, and state levels. His most recent appointment was as the founding president of the Ohio Principals Leadership Academy. He is past vice president of the American Educational Research Association (AERA) and was the founding chair of the Interstate School Leaders Licensure Consortium (ISLLC). He is coeditor of the AERA *Handbook on Educational Administration* (1999) and editor of the National Society for the Study of Education (NSSE) yearbook, *The Educational Leadership Challenge* (2002).

His work is in the area of school improvement, with special emphasis on leadership and policy. He has authored or coauthored twenty-one books in this area and edited another twelve. His most recent authored volumes include *Turning Around Failing Schools: Leadership Lessons from the Organizational Sciences* (2008), *The Educator's Handbook for Understanding and Closing Achievement Gaps* (2010), *Homelessness Comes to School* (2011), *Leadership Lessons for School Leaders* (2011), and *Homeschooling in America* (2012).

TALES OF SCHOOL IMPROVEMENT

The Mournful Tale of the Death of Mr. School Improvement

The Case of the Remarkable Reappearance of Mr. School Improvement

and

The Return of Mr. School Improvement

THE MOURNFUL TALE OF THE DEATH OF MR. SCHOOL IMPROVEMENT

It was exactly at 10:40 a.m. that Mrs. Wilson found the corpse of Mr. School Improvement on the cafeteria floor. Mrs. Wilson, the volunteer coordinator at William Burnett Middle School, was on her way to get a "bite to eat" before the first-lunch-period students arrived. Generally, this daily trip was fairly mundane, and usually Burnett was a pretty normal school. You will, I think, not be surprised to learn that the experience of discovering the corpse of Mr. School Improvement had an unsettling effect on poor Mrs. Wilson. She immediately, and with considerable celerity, set off to find Dr. Johnson, the interim principal of Burnett. Unfortunately, Dr. Johnson was the third interim principal at the school in the last two years. He hardly knew his way around the building yet and certainly didn't understand the approved pathway of action for dealing with a corpse in the school, especially one as famous as Mr. School Improvement. He did have the good sense to dispatch one of the deans to ensure that no students were permitted into the cafeteria until this issue was "addressed." He then called his boss, the superintendent of the Franklin School District, who informed him that she was immediately sending the district's three best forensic school improvement investigators—and would call the coroner as well.

As promised, within three minutes Barnabus Dolphin, Mr. Wolf (no first name), and C.B. (initials only) checked in at the office and hurriedly made their way to the Burnett cafeteria, sans administrative entourage. C.B. was the first to speak.

"Pretty unpleasant business," he said.

"Indeed," said Barnabus. "But perhaps it isn't as bad as Mrs. Wilson suggests. She always was the jittery type."

Any such hope quickly dissolved as the three detectives entered the cafeteria, after asking the dean to remain as sentinel.

"You were correct, C.B.," said Wolf. "Very bad business indeed. Dead without question."

"It is hard to believe that it is really our old friend," said Barnabus. "I haven't seen him in two or three years. He looks terrible. He was just a young man when last we met, and a big strapping fellow at that."

"Good fishmonger," echoed C.B. "Poor Mr. School Improvement looks like an old man."

"He is all worn down," chimed in Wolf.

"Let's see what is in his pockets," said C.B. "There may be a clue or two there."

A thorough search of Mr. School Improvement's corpse uncovered only one large envelope, in the inside pocket of his sports jacket.

"Hmmm, let's see what we have here," Barnabus remarked in an inquiring kind of way. "It is a large stack of FedEx delivery receipts."

"Odd, I think," murmured Wolf.

"Let me see those," said Barnabus in a reaching kind of way. "Just as I suspected. There are receipts here for twenty-five or thirty reform packages delivered to Mr. School Improvement at Burnett over the last half dozen years, a good ten or twelve arriving in the last eighteen months alone. There's one for a block scheduling kit and another for a student advisory system. And here's one for an interdisciplinary-based inquiry program and one for a detracking plan."

"Good fishmonger," cried out C.B. "Here are receipts for the delivery of a comprehensive school reform model and an entire small school. They must have been pretty large boxes."

"And here is a recent one for something called turnaround elixir," said Wolf. "Are you guys thinking what I'm thinking?"

Two confirmatory nods.

"He seemed to be getting more desperate," said C.B.

"And less coherent," said Barnabus.

"That 'Hail Mary' strategy never works," lamented Wolf. "His back must have really been up against the wall. Such a bad end to such a promising start for our friend."

Just then the coroner arrived on the scene, looking a good deal like "Doc" from the *Gunsmoke* series.

"Hi Doc," the three detectives nodded in unison. "Thanks for coming so quickly."

"My job," said the coroner, nodding in return. "Besides, being a school and all I thought we best get this cleared up as quickly as possible. Who is he?"

"His name is School Improvement," replied C.B. "Been at Burnett about eight years now as I recall."

"Whoa," said Doc, "I'm not used to seeing senior citizens in middle schools."

"Ah, but that's part of the rub," said Wolf. "He's really only a young man."

"Hmmm," said the coroner. "Best be having a look."

In the meantime, Wolf and Barnabus went to have a word with the sentinel (i.e., the dean). They asked him to call down and have Dr. Johnson convene an emergency meeting of the school leadership team for the second lunch period. They had questions. They needed some answers.

"And make sure Johnson orders pizza for everyone," Wolf stressed to the dean as they returned to join the coroner, who was just finishing up his examination of Mr. School Improvement.

"Well, Doc?" inquired C.B.

"Poor guy is pretty beaten up," said Doc. "Look here, his entire body is covered with small bruises and thin cuts. Layered on over a long stretch of time, I'd say. And look here," he pointed, "there is quite a number of larger contusions as well."

"My, my," said Barnabus. "We have not come up against that before in the district."

"No indeed," responded Wolf. "Nothing quite this bad, anyway. What's the cause of death, Doc?"

"That's the most peculiar part of the story," noted Doc. "Your friend, Mr. School Improvement, bled to death. Best I can tell he's been bleeding very slowly for quite a long time now. Hardly noticeable at any particular point in time but lethal over the long haul, as we see here," he reported in a puzzled kind of way. "Well, my people will be here shortly now and we'll get him downtown for an autopsy. Know for sure then," he reported.

The three district investigators then headed off for the teachers' lounge where Dr. Johnson had gathered together the twelve members of the school leadership team, per their request.

"Thank you all for coming on such short notice," began Wolf. "Know it is inconvenient, but we need your help. Has Dr. Johnson filled you all in? Good. We will get right to it, then," he explained with a nod to C.B.

"Thank you again for coming," said C.B. "We will get you back to your students just as fast as possible. Which of you knew the deceased the best?"

After some hesitation and a good deal of eye movement back and forth, Mrs. Peterson began. "A number of us were here when Mr. School Improvement came to Burnett. Let's see, that would have been seven or eight years ago. All of us know him, some better than others. But I'm pretty sure none of the teachers who came in the last three or four years know him well at all."

"How did he get here?" asked Barnabus.

"We invited him," answered Mrs. Guimond. "Voted as a full faculty actually."

"Any objections?" inquired Wolf.

"No, not really," said Mrs. Guimond. "We knew he was a good friend of the superintendent; probably in our best interest all around if you know what I mean."

Unmistakable glances of acknowledgment followed throughout the room.

"Many of us were generally excited about his joining us at Burnett," added Mrs. Fitzgerald. "Even the most jaded of us didn't really see much downside. No real problem potential."

"Hmmm," murmured Barnabus. "How did he fit in? Did he get along with everyone all right?"

"Oh yes," answered Mrs. Joy. "You know, when he came he brought a lot of extra stuff with him. You know, books, money for professional development trips, science equipment, stuff like that. And some things we really need at Burnett too. He was always around. You saw Mr. School Improvement pretty much everywhere. Very helpful. Sat in on all the leadership team meetings, right at the table with the rest of us. And most of the department meetings as well. He was an attractive devil for sure and we were drawn to him," she added in a blushing kind of way. "Seemed to have a lot of money, too, which didn't hurt."

"He was at all the administrative team meetings also," said Ms. Raschner. "I was an interim AP when he first came. Got along real well with the principal too."

"From what we can tell, and the coroner's initial investigation of the corpse, it seems pretty clear that things were not going well here at the end for Mr. School Improvement," said C.B.

"Yes, yes, that's true," said Mrs. Peterson. "Mrs. McCray had tried to alert us to possible problems way back at the start, when Mr. Improvement first came. Said she had worked with his brother at one school and his sister at another. Neither of those cases turned out well at all. She was clearly the most skeptical of all of us. Told us to keep our eyes open—and our 'doors closed.' Always was talking about the 'past returning again.' Smart woman that Mrs. McCray."

"And you know," said Mrs. Fitzgerald, "he grew more tiresome and bothersome the longer he was here," she reported in a somewhat annoyed but embarrassed kind of way. "He was kind of a my way or the highway type of guy. I never really had a sense that he understood much about Burnett. At least I never saw him make much effort to do so. Kind of knew everything already."

"Yeah, that's right," Mrs. Joy acknowledged. "He brought a whole bunch of stuff from Caldwell Elementary School, where he was before. A lot of it didn't seem to fit. Ended up in the closet. Still there, I believe."

C.B. gave a knowing nod to his colleagues. In their archaeological work in school closets throughout the district, they had uncovered more than their fair share of evidence to support Mrs. Joy's hunch.

A bit of a twinkle appeared in Barnabus's eyes and just a trace of a smile.

"Anything else?" said Wolf. "Did Mr. School Improvement have any friends?"

"Well, he was real tight with the superintendent at the time," said Mr. Rubio. "The guy before the guy before the current superintendent. Thick as thieves," he added in an inside kind of way.

"Not so much now though," added Mrs. Peterson. "The superintendent brought in a whole new team—you know, new ideas, new people, new ways of doing business. Even redid the district organizational chart. Not much space for Mr. School Improvement and his friends there, I'm told."

A meaningful glance was exchanged between Barnabus and C.B.— only an eyebrow movement, but clearly sufficient for two of the nation's foremost forensic school improvement investigators.

"What about with the teachers?" asked Barnabus.

"At first, he was liked by nearly everyone. Lots of friends, in a professional sense at least," replied Mrs. Jeffries. "You'd see him all the time in classrooms and hallways. Hung out a lot before and after school as well."

"What about now?" Barnabus asked in a probing kind of way.

"Things seem to have changed quite a bit," said Mrs. Peterson. "I know he still had a few friends in the AVID program, and he gets along with some of the social studies teachers."

"He really has become quite the loner," said Mrs. McCray. "We hardly see him anymore. Spends most of his time in his office putting together binders on all sorts of things. I was in there the other day looking for him. He had promised to get me a sub so I could observe Mrs. Guimond's science lesson. But since no sub ever came, I went down to see what the story was."

More nuanced eyebrow movements from the three forensic sleuths.

"He wasn't there. I was told he was at his regular meeting with some foundation at the district office. But his office was stuffed with stacks of really hefty binders. I remember that some were on his desk. One was on 'data,' another even bigger one on 'teacher quality,' and a monster-sized one on 'teacher evaluation.' Now that I think back on it, it seems odd that there weren't any binders on the children."

"Peculiar indeed," mused Wolf. "Anything else that you can tell us that might throw some light on the cause of Mr. School Improvement's demise? Any recent activity?"

After a bit of silence, Mrs. Fitzgerald spoke up. "Well," she said.

An informed nod among the three detectives indicated that they had some sense of where the narrative was heading.

"Well," Mrs. Fitzgerald repeated, "as Mrs. McCray reported, he had become almost a hermit, and I believe the situation was getting even worse.

We heard that Mr. School Improvement wasn't even getting along with the social studies teachers any longer, and we all know that that is hard to do."

"You know he had promised quite a lot when he came to Burnett," said Mrs. Joy. "And as we said, he seemed to have a lot of money, at least a lot more than any of us had ever seen."

"You know we still got stuff from time to time," said Mr. Rubio. "But we didn't really know what to do with most of it."

"And even when we did," chimed in Mrs. Peterson, "when it broke there wasn't really anyone to help fix stuff. We tried working on broken stuff in small groups for a while, but that petered out. Too much other stuff to do, I guess."

"More and more of us just pulled away," Mrs. Guimond reported, in an embarrassed but defiant kind of way. "You know, just closed our doors and went on with our work."

"Hmmm," whispered C.B.

Mrs. Joy jumped in here. "I also don't think that he had the ear of the new interim principal, Dr. Johnson. It wasn't like they were at each other's throats, though. I just don't think they understood each other. In the old days, Mr. School Improvement and the interim principals always seemed to be together. We don't see that anymore."

"All true," nodded Ms. Raschner, the school psychologist, in a meaningful kind of way. "But there is more here, I believe. I don't think he saw himself as particularly successful. Even when things worked in one or two classes, they didn't seem to take off. I think this really ate at him. He aged right before our eyes."

"And grew less and less pleasant, too," said Mr. Rubio. "Meaner and more pushy, I would say."

"Oh my," said Barnabus, exchanging knowing looks with his forensic partners.

"At the last faculty meeting he told us that he had 'friends in high places,' insinuating that they were right at the top of the educational food chain in Washington."

"He snarled at us," said Mrs. Fitzgerald. "Told us that if things didn't begin to shape up around here, 'heads would roll.' Said we would all find ourselves 'out on the street.' The words still ring in my ears."

"He even threatened to sell the entire school to the Smoogle Hat Company," chimed in Mrs. Guimond. "Very unpleasant."

It was at this point that they saw the corpse of Mr. School Improvement being conveyed to the waiting ambulance.

"Well, I think we have enough for now," Wolf reported in a gracious kind of way. "My colleagues and I want to thank you again for your help with this investigation. We are in your debt—as is the district and the education industry in general," he closed.

Later that afternoon we find the three renowned forensic school improvement sleuths at afternoon tea at their local House of Coffee.

"You look glum, my friend," said Wolf to C.B.

"It is this unpleasant business with Mr. School Improvement," he replied. "I can't seem to shake it."

"Me either," said Barnabus. "Even though it is becoming increasingly common, it's still sad."

"I just don't get the sense that he really knew what he was doing—and where he was going, for that matter," lamented C.B. in a mournful and disappointed kind of way. "And moving faster and working harder didn't seem to help much."

"Yes, he covered an amazing amount of territory but didn't seem to really go very far," said Wolf.

"And he irritated pretty much everyone to boot," added C.B. "Just another layer of organizational sediment at Burnett, I guess."

"And the nonnourishing kind," said Wolf in a faraway kind of voice.

"Let's all have a piece of cinnamon swirl pound cake," said Barnabus. "It is good for chasing away school improvement ghosts and glumness."

"What do you think will happen to the body?" inquired Barkley, the store manager, who was refreshing their drinks and laying out the pound cake.

"I dropped by Mr. School Improvement's attorney's office earlier this afternoon to see if I could get an answer to that very question," said Wolf. "Turns out he asked for his body to be cremated and for his ashes to be spread on the lawn of the State Department of Education. But I wouldn't worry too much. It turns out our friend Mr. School Improvement was a firm believer in reincarnation. So I suspect we will be seeing him again downstream."

THE CASE OF THE REMARKABLE REAPPEARANCE OF MR. SCHOOL IMPROVEMENT

The last time we saw the three forensic school improvement detectives it was in regard to the case of the death of Mr. School Improvement at Burnett Middle School some six years ago. As we join them again, they are just finishing their mocha frappacinos and double berry bran muffins at their local House of Coffee.

"Well," reported Wolf, "Barnabus and I need to get back to the office to finish up our report on the collapse of parent advisory councils in the district, and you, C.B., are needed at Central High School, if I am not mistaken."

"Yes," mulled C.B. "It looks like the entire interdisciplinary curriculum units initiative is under water. I believe that Mrs. Welch, the principal, was too greatly smitten with that report from the August Captains of Industry (ACI) about the imminent demise of the Carnegie unit."

"Hmmm," retorted Wolf. "I remember, a pretty scathing critique of the American education system, but perhaps just a tad premature on their prediction for the elimination of the Carnegie unit."

"Yes, indeed," chimed in Barnabus, in a historically anchored kind of way. "In the last seventy-five years, that old Carnegie unit has been shown the door more times that I can count. But the cheeky old codger never seems to take the hint. Every school year he is back at the head of the table."

"Well, I'll go have a look," said C.B. "See what the story is this time. Perhaps the Central High initiative can be salvaged yet."

The three sleuths bused their table and headed off to their assigned tasks.

When Wolf and Barnabus were settled in their office at the Franklin Board of Education building, they pulled out their nearly finished report: *Fuzzy Logic, Faulty Conventional Wisdom, Discredited Science, and Bad Data: The Collapse of School-Based Parent Advisory Councils in the Franklin School District.* They just needed to complete the executive summary and ship the completed document off to their boss before calling it a day and heading home to the condominium that they shared with C.B.

"It's too bad," lamented Wolf, "it really is. Everyone at the top thought this one was a winner for sure. The predecessor of the current superintendent four times removed pushed it really hard. Even got the teachers' union to sign on. Carried a parcel of district and community bigwigs up to Chicago and Kentucky to see it in action."

Barnabus allowed as he recalled that time well. "The corporate community was certainly on board in a big way," he noted. "Said it would solve all manner of problems, everything from the antiquated school calendar to the absence of accountability. According to the written report, it was to be 'the hub of a carousel of progress.'"

"Hmmm," responded Wolf, "an uplifting document for sure, but with claims that were perhaps just a bit optimistic."

"Perhaps," snarled Barnabus. "The principals I have spoken to were spending more time calling parents and begging them to come to council meetings than they were leading those meetings. They rarely got a quorum, and when they did, it was generally different people."

"Well," ruminated Wolf, "we have done all we can on this case. Add the introduction, Barnabus, and e-mail the report to the boss and we'll be off for home."

When they arrived home they discovered C.B. lying on his back on the couch holding a copy of the *Scientific Bulletin of School Improvement Forensics* in one hand and using the other to steady an ice pack on his head.

"What is the problem?" asked Barnabus, for his good friend C.B. was looking anything but well.

"It's Mr. School Improvement," sputtered C.B. "He's back."

"Hmmm," remarked Wolf. "I don't believe this augurs well for the district, or for education in general for that matter."

"How is that possible?" asked Barnabus. "We saw his corpse at Burnett School."

"It's happened before," responded Wolf in a knowing kind of way. "Almost all his relatives have reappeared after their initial demise. You remember Mrs. Homogenous Grouping, Dr. Inquiry-Based Learning, Ms. Phonics, and Mr. Alternative Schedule? It seems the family has the ability to reincarnate."

"Holy fishmonger," cried Barnabus. "Where did you see him?"

"He has a full-page ad in the new issue of the *Scientific Bulletin of School Improvement Forensics*," said C.B., waving his copy of the journal. "And he was on the television. Although now he is calling himself Dr. School Improvement."

"More nefarious shenanigans in our colleges of education," remarked Wolf sternly. "A bit of overreach for students, I'm afraid, if they found room for Mr. School Improvement."

"I recorded his TV ad," C.B. interrupted. "You can see for yourselves."

"We'd best fortify ourselves for this with some cold milk and cookies," said Barnabus, already headed for the kitchen.

When the three intrepid investigators were all comfortably ensconced on the sofa, with milk and cookies in easy reach, C.B. mashed on the control. A very robust-looking Mr. School Improvement appeared on the screen wearing a lab coat and carrying a thick binder of what looked to be research studies on school improvement. This clearly was not the wizened and enfeebled corpse that they had seen being toted out of Burnett Middle School on a stretcher for a trip to the morgue.

"Hello," began our reincarnated friend. "My name is Dr. School Improvement. I am the founder and CEO of the company that brings you Failure Be Gone™."

"Ouch," mumbled Wolf. "I don't like how this is taking shape at all."

Mr. (Dr.) School Improvement was beaming from the TV screen. "Failure Be Gone™," he continued, "is a revolutionary new product, developed by our team of scientists in our own laboratories. It is a real game changer for struggling schools."

"Do you think that is possible?" inquired Barnabus.

"Highly implausible," responded Wolf. "Let's see what else our old friend has to say for himself."

"I know that many of you have tried other failure elimination products in the past," continued Mr. School Improvement. "And I know that you frequently have been disappointed with the results. But Failure Be Gone™ is different. It is a transformational invention built from documented best practices. It has been scientifically proven in rigorous research studies to eliminate failure at every level of schooling and in every type of community!" he exclaimed excitedly while waving his binder of evidence enthusiastically.

"It also comes with an ironclad guarantee," he continued. "If for any reason Failure Be Gone™ does not work as promised, the FBG Company will provide you at no cost with three jumbo binders stuffed with an assortment of school improvement materials—plans, curriculum audit materials, climate surveys, and much, much more."

"Hmmm," interjected Barnabus. "I guess I assumed that if Mr. School Improvement ever did come back, he would return a wiser man."

"And given his checkered past, a more humble one, I had hoped," said C.B.

"The positive evidence on both fronts looks to be exceptionally thin at this point," Wolf weighed in. "Let's hope that the district office folks did not see this ad. They have pretty short memories, and this is exactly the kind of product that they would find appealing."

"Indeed," Barnabus summed up. "They seem to be on a constant quest for the fountain of school reform."

Mr. School Improvement was back in action, lab coat flapping and binder waiving. "Before we turn to a testimonial from one of our exceptionally pleased clients, we are obligated to note some of the possible negative effects associated with the use of Failure Be Gone™. My associate, Ms. Systemic School Reform, will overview these issues for you."

"Thank you, Dr. School Improvement," nodded Ms. Systemic School Reform. "As you well know," she went on, "all improvement interventions have potential negative consequences. Side effects for Failure Be Gone™ include conflict, disengagement and reduced commitment, lowered morale, reduced sense of efficacy (individual and collective), withdrawal (people hiding in plain sight), scapegoating and blaming, nervousness, and pasty-looking skin color. In some cases, Failure Be Gone™ has been associated with meanness, severe weight loss, the centralization of power, severe weight gain, dizziness and fainting, fatigue, muscle spasms, numbness of the heart and soul, retaliation, and a glazed-over zombie-like appearance. In a not insignificant number of cases, the use of Failure Be Gone™ has resulted in addiction to improvement initiatives, loss of trust, dismissal, total collapse of the school, and death. If you experience any of these conditions, stop using Failure Be Gone™ and notify your superintendent."

"Hmmm," interjected Wolf. "There seems to be a bit of a downside here, my friends."

"A bit," blurted out C.B. "I wonder how Mr. School Improvement got this product rushed onto the market so quickly. The Reform Implementation Administration must have been asleep at the wheel."

"Maybe him being a doctor now helped somehow," conjectured Barnabus.

"Thank you, Ms. Systemic School Reform," nodded Mr. School Improvement. "I think everyone can see that the risks with using Failure Be Gone™ are minimal while the upside is tremendous."

"We just have time to hear from one of our highly satisfied clients in the time remaining," he went on. "Dr. Willite would like to say a few words," he interjected, before handing the microphone to a well-dressed and perky-looking woman in her mid-40s.

"My goodness," blurted out C.B. "That is Dr. Willite. She was the principal at Franklin West Middle School about 15 years ago, if my memory is working."

"Correct," Barnabus asserted. "Invested a good deal of energy working with the Middle Brain Institute on an extensive program on identifying and teaching to students' learning styles. And her school was one of the first to adopt 'the building esteem to promote learning' program as well."

"That's right," responded Wolf. "The results, I believe, were a bit disappointing all the way round. She completed her doctorate and was moved to one of the high schools to implement the program there, I think."

"Right, Wombley Alternative High School," Barnabus filled in. "Same results there, though, I'm afraid."

The attention of the three detectives returned to the television, where Dr. Willite was starting to speak.

"Well, my friends," she began, "I just can't say enough about Failure Be Gone™. We tried one failure elimination product after another. Sometimes failure went away for a while but he always managed to find his way back. All that changed, however, the day the FedEx truck brought us our box of Failure Be Gone™. We couldn't be happier. Everyone at the school feels like a new person. The entire school community has been rejuvenated. We simply wait for the youngsters to fall two years below grade level. Then we move all our resources from other initiatives and pour them into the Failure Be Gone™ plan. We all feel like we are poised for success now."

"Of course, our student achievement scores have gone down the first two years," Dr. Willite continued. "But Dr. School Improvement helped us see that this was to be expected, something he describes as the implementation dip. Nothing to worry about, he told us. Things should start to turn around soon now, especially since we invested so much money last year in the Failure Be Gone™ professional development and technology and have hired a full-time Failure Be Gone™ coach."

"Wow," explained C.B., "that Mr. School Improvement is quite the salesman."

"Perhaps just a bit too good," remarked Wolf.

"Well folks, there you have it," said Mr. School Improvement. "Failure Be Gone™—a 100% successful formula for school improvement. Thousands of boxes have been sold to schools throughout the nation".

"Oh my," mumbled Barnabus. "This is in thousands of schools already. And many more on the way, looks like."

Wolf just rolled his eyes and scowled.

"And if you order today," continued Mr. School Improvement, "we have a special gift for you. To help you on your path to becoming a data-driven school, with your box of Failure Be Gone™ we will ship two thumb drives of data. If you order in the next fifteen minutes, we will also include one of our patented school improvement binders, one chock-full of great information."

"I think that's about enough of this!" exclaimed C.B. while polishing off the last cookie. "Something tells me that all this is likely to go up in smoke in a few years. And I don't think we have seen the end of our old friend Mr. School Improvement quite yet."

"I'm afraid that is exceedingly likely to be the case on both fronts," said Wolf in a meditative kind of way.

THE RETURN OF MR. SCHOOL IMPROVEMENT

It was nearly five years ago that we last saw the three sagacious forensic school improvement sleuths, Mr. Wolf, Barnabus Dolphin, and C.B. They had just witnessed the remarkable reappearance of Mr. School Improvement and the worrisome introduction of his newest reform product, Failure Be Gone™. Since that time, they had had almost no news of their old friend. They were aware, of course, of the meteoric rise and equally precipitous fall of Failure Be Gone™, both the product and the company, but of Mr. School Improvement himself little was known. The most credible information available suggested that he had seen the errors of his ways and was working to rebuild schools in Central America.

As we reconnect with the three detectives, we find them conducting an archaeological exploration of the main storage closet at Joseph Sinnott Elementary School. They had begun their assignment in the rear of the closet long before the teachers and students arrived at school. By 2:15 p.m., they had worked their way nearly 80% of the way toward the door, providing an informed analysis of school improvement work in Sinnott (and the nation) over the last half century.

"This is interesting," shouted out Barnabus. "Here is a large box of *Hands On Science Activities*. Do you recall similar material from this morning?"

"Indeed I do," replied C.B. "From the 1960s era, I tagged some *COPES* science units and whole sets of inquiry-based science materials from the 1980s. All seemed as if they had hardly been used though."

"Hmmm," said Mr. Wolf, carefully lifting various objects with his gloved paws. "Here is a *Phonics Is Fun* program, pretty dog-eared too. And just a few shelves closer to the front are boxes of books with warning labels indicating 'no phonics allowed.'"

"Oh my," noted Barnabus, "these warning labels have been defaced. And it isn't children's writing. I'd bet my pension on that."

"Look here, we are entering the era when Mr. School Improvement began his most recent school reform efforts," said C.B. "Here is an entire shelf of Failure be Gone™."

"Let me have a closer look," nodded Barnabus. "As I suspected. These boxes have never even been opened."

"Probably for the best anyway," interjected Mr. Wolf. "I think our schools would be better off if the school improvement crowd honored their credo of 'do no harm.'"

A step or two closer to the door and tucked behind boxes of authentic learning assessments they espied Mr. School Improvement's trilogy of school reform books.

"I remember these well," said C.B., "best sellers all. The district purchased a set for every principal. Everyone on pins and needles waiting for a subsequent volume to appear."

"They organized book clubs around them too" Mr. Wolf interjected. "Let me see them," he requested, in a reaching kind of way.

Book one featured a bank on the cover and was titled *Buying Your Way to School Improvement.*

"Nice endorsements on the cover from all sorts of important government figures," said Wolf. "Book two is titled *Trust No One: Do It Yourself* and features a smiling portrait of Mr. School Improvement himself," he continued. "Oh, and here is the final volume, the massive best seller that took school administration by storm: *Bludgeoning Your Way to Effectiveness: You Can't Buy School Improvement.*"

"A bit contradictory, I'd argue," reported Barnabus. "Isn't that the one in which SI argues that teachers don't really care about kids—and that they are kind of lazy?" he asked.

"Indeed," retorted C.B. "He generated a good deal of mischief with that one, for sure."

C.B. and Barnabus looked up to see Wolf with a faraway look on his face, abstractly tapping on his watch.

"I was just entertaining a notion that since we worked through lunch and because my belly is grumbling fast and hard that we all might be advantaged by a visit to the House of Coffee," said Wolf.

"Really a capital suggestion," chimed in C.B., unbuckling his school improvement tool belt and carefully laying aside his school improvement age spectrometer.

When they arrived at the local House of Coffee, they ordered three venti vanilla lattes and pieces of cinnamon swirl, pumpkin, and lemon-blueberry pound cake, each cut into three chunks. You will not be surprised to learn that their conversation flowed naturally into the well-grooved channel of school improvement. Specifically, talk focused on tentative lessons learned from their archaeological explorations at Sinnott School and the alignment of those insights with the larger body of their findings on school improvement.

"I've been puzzling this through," said Barnabus, with a touch of pride in his voice, "and based on all of our investigations, I think I've created a pretty good model of school improvement that can shape our future work."

An affirming glance and nod between Wolf and C.B. confirmed their respect and admiration for their friend and colleague.

Just as the detectives began to pore over the ideas outlined by Barnabus Dolphin, they were interrupted by their friend Barkley (the manager of the House of Coffee), who was shouting that Mr. School Improvement was a minute away from appearing on a breaking news story, one that would feature the mayor of Zolator and the governor of Yolbit as well.

"Hmmm," noted Mr. Wolf. "The last time we heard from SI he distressed our ears somewhat unmercifully. If we are to survive this, we'd best have another round of coffee and more pound cake as well, I think."

The advertisement that Barkley had been shouting over came to an end and a reporter appeared on screen announcing that he was following a breaking news story in the city of Zolator. The camera panned in on two beefy, middle-aged men, the mayor of Zolator and the governor of Yolbit, standing at an outside podium in front of a collection of reporters and camerapersons.

"Good afternoon, everyone," began Mayor Jeffries. "As you are all aware, the Zolator Unified School District has gone through some pretty rough times over the last few decades. Enrollments have plummeted. There has been a steady decline in test scores. Attendance and graduation rates have fallen a good deal. Morale is on a downward trajectory. Leadership has been in short supply. And community support and involvement are at historic lows."

"For the last year, Governor Backman and I, with considerable help from civic and business leaders, have been working diligently to find someone to help us break this cycle of decline, to create a district that works for each child and a school system of which we can all be proud. We are here today to inform you that we have found our person. Let me introduce the new superintendent of the Zolator Unified School District, Dr. School Improvement."

"Hmmm," murmured Wolf, with a mouthful of pumpkin pound cake. "Let's see if our old friend has learned anything since we saw him last."

"Hello," said Mr. School Improvement, in an acknowledging kind of way. "It will be an honor to become the new superintendent of the Zolator District this summer. With the support of Mayor Jeffries and Governor Backman, I look forward to turning around the sixth largest district in the nation."

"Can I answer any questions at this time?"

A reporter from the middle of the crowd yelled out, "What is the plan, Dr. School Improvement? How are you going to pull this off? Will Failure Be Gone™ be featured?"

"Thank you," replied Mr. School Improvement. "I have learned a good deal about change over the last forty years of my career, too much of it, I might acknowledge, through some not-so-good decisions. So my immediate plan is to ask my three old friends, the three most respected forensic school improvement detectives in the country, to come to Zolator and help the district lay out a roadmap for success. We have allotted two months this spring to get the work done. I will be contacting them as soon as we are done here."

"Oh my," said C.B. in a choking and startled kind of way.

"Another round of pound cake is required, please, Barkley," Wolf hollered across the din of the room.

The news conference went on for nearly an hour. Mr. School Improvement, Mayor Jeffries, and Governor Backman all took turns at the podium as required. When the affair had ended, optimism scented the air. People felt buoyed.

Perhaps the fall had indeed been broken, the bleeding stanched, and the corner turned, thought each of the three detectives independently and collectively.

Just then, a familiar ding rang out on Mr. Wolf's phone. It was a text from Mr. School Improvement:

Come with all due haste. Bring C.B. and Barnabus. Important work to be done in the next two months. Your presence critical and your wisdom essential. SI

Two days have passed and we now rejoin the three sleuths in the office of Mr. School Improvement in the Zolator District building. The usual pleasantries and greetings have already taken place by the time we join the meeting. Knowing of the detectives' proclivity for pastries, the superintendent has provided a large plate of assorted muffins and two pitchers of sweet tea.

"Pretty tiny office for the superintendent of the nation's sixth largest school district, don't you think?" said C.B., bringing the meeting to point.

"I selected this one on purpose," replied Mr. School Improvement. "Didn't want to create the impression of being more important than others," he continued. "It really is about the collective effort, you know. And given the context of the district, I thought this move made sense."

Raised eyebrows from Wolf and Barnabus, in an approving kind of way though.

"How can we help?" inquired Mr. Wolf, focusing the meeting even more tightly.

"Well," replied the soon-to-be superintendent, "during the two days it took you guys to drive up here, I've been working on a plan to propel school improvement here in Zolator. I really would appreciate your feedback on the design I've come up with. You know, let me know if you think it can work."

"Shoot," encouraged C.B.

Mr. School Improvement was aglow with enthusiasm. "Well," he commenced, "the plan has three very distinct parts and I am pretty excited about each of them."

A tiny trace of a frown became visible on the face of each detective, undetectable to all but other forensic sleuths.

"As you know," Mr. School Improvement began, "I've collaborated pretty closely in the past with the Middle Brain Institute. Their new project on working memory is very appealing. I am entertaining a notion of having all the teachers and administrators take their one-week training session this August, before school begins. The brain as a muscle. Pretty cool, don't you think?" he concluded.

C.B. shuffled uncomfortably in his seat and was about to offer some insights on the matter when Wolf offered him the plate of muffins and asked that Mr. School Improvement please complete the narrative on his tentative plan.

"Well, we received a boatload of money from the state and the feds," he resumed. "So, I'm thinking we should conduct some empirical research right here in Zolator. Use random assignment and include all the bells and whistles."

It was now Barnabus's turn to be offered the plate of muffins.

"Please proceed," said Mr. Wolf.

"Right now," the superintendent went on, "we have PK–8 schools and 9–12 schools. It seems like a really good idea if we change that," he nodded excitedly. "I think we should reset the structure, go to PK–2, 3–5, 6–8, and 9–12 schools. I'm anticipating all manner of positive benefits from this particular change."

Mr. School Improvement was surprised when the three forensic detectives failed to provide the spontaneous approbation he had expected. A troubled countenance emerged.

Mr. Wolf coughed in a polite kind of way and replaced his glass of sweet tea on the table. "SI," he began, "we can see that you have discovered some important lessons about leading school improvement and put them into play here in Zolator even before you officially begin this summer. It is also clear, however, that you still have a good deal to learn. None of these three initiatives will do anything to improve your schools, my friend," he said in a stern yet comforting manner. "And given all that you have been through, you of all people should know better."

"Yes, yes, of course. I see that now," said the crestfallen superintendent. "I've fallen back into some less-than-productive routines, I'm afraid. What can we do that will really help the district, that can productively direct everyone on the school improvement journey?"

"Well," Mr. Wolf responded with a shared glance with his colleagues, "the three of us were talking about that a good bit on the trip here. Based on some initial designs that Barnabus has created, we believe that we can put our collective wisdom—ours and yours, SI—into a form that can accomplish that very objective, a guidebook that steers folks away from making poor decisions and toward productive ones."

"Wow, that sounds really great," Mr. School Improvement replied in an almost agitated manner. "When can we start?"

"We already have," C.B. jumped in. "We have arranged for a two-month sabbatical for us, and you have two months before you officially take over. During that time, the four of us will capture everything your folks will need to know in a guidebook on school improvement. Barnabus says we should lay out the broad picture to start and then focus on the key principles that school people need to follow to do the work of school improvement well."

"Barnabus, you are a sleuth of distinction," said Mr. S.I. "Let's start with the broad picture, then a model, perhaps, and work our way out."

FRAMEWORK FOR SCHOOL IMPROVEMENT

The assignment in this brief section is to present a way of thinking about school improvement that grounds its conclusions on the best empirical evidence from the last three decades. We lay out a framework that accomplishes this in five parts: An essential equation, building material, construction principles, enabling supports, and an integrative device (see Figure 1).

The Essential School Improvement Equation

Collectively, the evidence directs us to the position that there is an essential school improvement algorithm, one that is both simple and elegant:

School Improvement = Academic Press + Supportive Community

The equation represents the core of school improvement work in the modern era. Another parsimonious model for this narrative is the double helix. Both encapsulations inform us that (1) these are the two critical components of school improvement; (2) they are most powerful in tandem; and (3) they work best when they wrap around each other like strands in a rope.

Building Material

The question at hand is this: How can academic press and supportive culture be created in schools; and how can school improvement be realized? Scholarship over the years leads to the conclusion that the answer is contained in the other pieces of the framework.

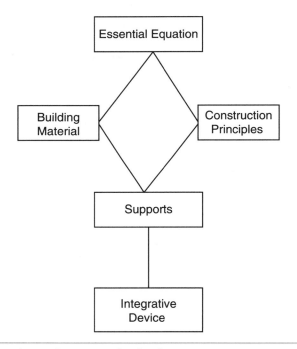

Figure 1 The Architecture of School Improvement

One of these pieces, the content, involves identifying and bringing the right materials to the school improvement building site. This is the aspect of the framework that has been most deeply explored over the last three decades. During that time, researchers have been quite active in mining for the raw materials of school improvement. In addition, using this material, numerous content-based taxonomies have been forged, beginning around 1980 with the correlates of effective schools and carrying through to today as seen in the recent comprehensive review of meta-analyses by Hattie (2009) and in the hallmark study by Bryk and colleagues (2010) on the essential elements of school improvement.

The good news here is that while lists and taxonomies often feature different terms and place ideas in different categories, there is an astonishing amount of agreement on the material contained in these categorizations, on the ingredients of school improvement, that is. Table 1 provides a taxonomy constructed from those studies, one that captures the "right stuff" of school improvement—the content with the potential to create academic press and supportive culture.

Table 1   The Building Material of School Improvement

Quality Instruction
- Effective teachers
- Quality pedagogy

Curriculum
- Content coverage
- Time
- Rigor
- Relevance

Personalized Learning Environment for Students
- Safe and orderly climate
- Meaningful connections
- Opportunities to participate

Professional Learning Environment for Educators
- Collaborative culture of work
- Participation and ownership
- Shared leadership

Learning-Centered Leadership
- Forging academic press
- Developing supportive culture

Learning-Centered Linkages to the School Community
- Connections to parents
- Linkages to community agencies and organizations

Monitoring of Progress and Performance Accountability
- Performance-based goals
- Systematic used of data
- Shared accountability

Construction Principles

While attention has been lavished on uncovering the best materials (content) to use to forge school improvement initiatives, that is, to help create schools defined by academic press and supportive culture, our understanding of the rules that need to be followed in putting the content pieces together is much less well developed. What we do know is often embedded in or threaded across the content narrative. Principles rarely have a starring role in the school improvement play. One often has to read between the lines to discover these ideas. The art of "seeing the missing" is also essential in developing an understanding of these guiding principles. Forensic school improvement work, as seen in the three tales of Mr. School Improvement, is generally a good method of identifying the pieces of this critical component of the model of school improvement.

Based on a close reading of school improvement research over a long period of time, it seems clear that construction principles are as important as the content elements in school improvement work. Working on the latter without attending to the former is a recipe for failure, akin to building beautiful rooms on the third floor of a house without load-bearing walls. This book focuses on these principles and essential lessons.

Supports

We also learn, again from examining embedded patterns in the school improvement mosaic, that "organizational tools" need to be thoughtfully used if school improvement efforts are to bear fruit. They are the fourth component of the framework.

All the building materials and guiding principles by definition carry a positive charge; each is a hero or heroine in the school improvement narrative, although, as we noted above, with limited powers when working alone. Organizational supports, on the other hand, are neutral. They can carry either a positive or negative charge; that is, they can be employed to help or hinder school improvement work.

There is a variety of ways to think about these supports or tools. For example, there is the well-established framework of "capital": human capital, financial capital, social capital, and so forth, with each form of capital comprised of numerous sub-dimensions (e.g., leadership capital in the human capital area). However, in employing the idea of "neutral charge," a design that is more compact and considerably less likely to bleed into "material" and "principles" than other support taxonomies is underscored. Included are organizational structures (e.g., grade-level academies, K–2 schools), operating systems (e.g., procedures for assigning children to teachers and classes), policies (e.g., assigning struggling students to mandatory afterschool tutoring), and practices (e.g., the way the principal interacts with children in the school hallways). There is considerable evidence in the school improvement research that the tools to mix quality material and construction principles in a productive fashion are found in these categories.

The Integrative Dynamic

Since the first studies of effective schools and districts and investigations of successful change, leadership has enjoyed a central role in the school improvement narrative. It is prominently displayed in Table 1. Work over the last twenty years takes us beyond that conclusion, however. A deeper pattern of leadership in the school improvement tapestry and a more central location for that pattern is discernible. The story line is one in which school leaders provide the dynamism to make all the components of the framework function. The recent cardinal volume by Bryk and colleagues (2010) affirms leadership as the integrative dynamic. More specifically, they conclude that leadership is the essential enabling element of school improvement work.

We turn in the rest of the book to an in-depth exploration of the principles or essential lessons of school improvement. As noted in the introduction, we scaffold these lessons around three tales of Mr. School Improvement and three forensic school improvement sleuths, Mr. Wolf, Barnabus Dolphin, and C.B.

ESSENTIAL LESSONS

THE LAW OF THE UNINVITED GUEST

At its best, school improvement will provide a school with real benefits. A variety of good things will walk in the front door. But goal achievement always means that there is the potential for bad things to walk in the back door as well. If these unintended consequences can be anticipated, they can either be barred from entry or defanged. Absent such work, they can cause a good deal of mischief. One has to look no further than the most visible reforms of the last decades—standards and accountability—to see that most of the profession ignored this lesson. We not only failed to lock the back door but left it open as well. In came a singular focus on bubble kids, the death of entire curricular domains (with some still surviving on life support), testing replacing curriculum, and so on. None of these consequences were inevitable. A little foresight would have gone a long way.

THE TENDENCY OF "RIGHTNESS"

Getting the organization to where it needs to be is more important than fighting over who is right. There is no need in school improvement work to bludgeon each other with reminders of brilliance. It sends an assortment of nonhelpful messages and dampens enthusiasm for investing energy in future school improvement work.

Source: Murphy (2011).

THE FORMULA OF BACKWARD MAPPING

Good school improvement work occurs when schools begin with the end in mind, backward mapping from where they want to be.

THE RULE OF CHALLENGES

Solving problems is a good thing for sure. But meeting challenges is better. The former is often deficit oriented and tinged with faultfinding. The latter is future oriented and colored with a sense of possibility.

THE DECREE OF ANSWERS

Many people in the school improvement world operate well in the abstract and in framing important questions. A curriculum of questions is useful. But school improvement requires a curriculum of answers. Schools don't improve in the abstract. School people need to see the nuts and bolts of the machinery. In addition, they need to be provided with the tools to do the work. And remember, philosophy is not a tool.

THE LAW OF THE DIP

People often develop unrealistic and damaging expectations about the slope of improvement. They expect what almost never happens, a fast start and upwardly moving line. As a result they often damage the very progress they wish to see develop. The great teachers in the area of school improvement help us see that things almost always trend downward before they begin to rise. This is the period in which high-magnitude mistakes (e.g., withdrawal, scapegoating) are especially apt to occur. Educators need to understand the law of the dip and manage change accordingly.

THE PRINCIPLES OF PROLIX

Language, especially lengthy exhortations and explanations, often washes over students and teachers, generally leaving little residue. This is especially the case when people are reluctant or adverse to making the school improvement trip. Actions trump words. Resistance cannot be talked away. It needs to be actively dismantled.

THE COMMUNITY SHARING CODE

Widespread change will be problematic if schools are expected to carry all the improvement freight themselves. Social capital from the larger community needs to be mixed with the school resources in a coherent manner.

THE DOCTRINE OF THE SECOND EYEBALL

It is easy in the midst of the school improvement journey to begin seeing the landscape, the people, the challenges, and so on the way you prefer that they be. Step back. Look again. Get another perspective. It wouldn't hurt to invite someone with fresh eyes to have a look too.

Source: Murphy (2011).

THE HOTHOUSE CAUTION

Many industries employ "hothouses" and "Skunk Works" to grow new improvements. Nurtured by a cadre of leaders and ferociously protected from the withering touch of bureaucracy, changes that take root are then transplanted to the rest of the organization where they routinely flourish. Attractive as they may appear, such strategies do not work well in education. Existing cultures kill young plants. The key for schools, as Michael Fullan continually reminds us, is reculturing the school so new ideas can develop.

THE RULE OF RESISTANCE

People engaged in school improvement efforts need to understand that resistance is normal, often occupying a large section of the change landscape. If resistance is normal, then we need to stop thinking of resisters as deviants or people possessed of major character flaws. Resistance is actually taught by schools and learned by teachers (and students). It has to be untaught and unlearned. And remember that telling is not teaching.

THE SOCIALIZATION LAPSE

A critical mistake in much school improvement work is the failure to account for new people (e.g., employees, customers) who enter endeavors after the work has started and often progressed a considerable distance. Information about why initiatives were begun may have gone missing. The work itself may appear ungrounded and without meaning. Unless action is taken to prevent it, the pool of the knowledgeable and committed will shrink. And the improvement work will slow and/or become isolated.

THE TRUTH ABOUT DISAGREEMENT

It is generally pleasant to be around people who agree with us. However, we need to remember that we are more likely to learn from those who disagree with us. The message: In school improvement work, we need to create a culture in which differences are legitimized.

Source: Murphy (2011).

THE TENET OF UP AND DOWN

Scholars have provided considerable wisdom over the last thirty years about the limitations of "single malt" improvement brews. They also have a good deal to say about the "power of up and down." Improvement initiatives work best when ideas and energy bubble up from the bottom and cascade down from the top.

THE LAW OF PERCEPTIONS

Perceptions are reality. They need to be acknowledged, not dismissed out of hand. Denigrating perceptions will not assist the improvement process. People need to see with their own eyes that their assessments merit alteration. This occurs as school improvement work opens them to other conclusions, not because of calls to see differently.

THE DOCTRINE OF RELATIONSHIPS

Improvement in schools has as much to do with relationships as it does with the goodness of the improvement efforts. Relationships open the door to improvement and sustain work when the inevitable problems and missteps occur.

THE LAW OF COMMITMENT

There are many ways to reach school improvement goals. Some will be technically better than others. But as Richard Elmore reminds us, commitment is the trump card. Things that people believe in, agree to work on collectively, and labor on with diligence tend to work well.

THE PRINCIPLE OF THE DEAF EAR

(and the Closed Eye)

Most people being asked to board the school improvement bus have been there before, often many times before. This is what they have learned. The bus may not start. If it does start, it may veer off course. Or break down. When things look like they might work, it is possible that someone will come along and change the mode of travel and the rules of the road. The benefits of making the trip are likely never to materialize. The riders, not surprisingly, become leery about additional travel. Their ears are clogged and their eyes are misted over. Attention to this reality at the start of a school improvement effort will be especially helpful. Ignoring it will cause trouble.

THE ORDINANCE OF BOUNDARIES

Schools need to agree up front on the boundaries in which the school improvement game will be played. Degrees of freedom exist inside but not outside that playing field.

Source: Murphy (2011).

THE MARTYR'S CREED

Many of the narratives of school improvement, especially in tough environments and with children who have been damaged, are tales of saints and martyrs, stories in which educators gave up their own lives in the service of young people. These are uplifting chronicles. But martyrdom is a nonreplicable model of school improvement. Whatever school improvement is undertaken needs to fit normal, hard-working teachers and administrators.

THE LAW OF EQUIFINALITY

Given the complexity in schools, the law of multiple pathways is in full force. School improvement initiatives need to affirm this truth, and not misspend limited capital constantly dragging everyone back to the one true pathway.

THE LAW OF ENTROPY

School improvement is subject to the law of entropy. Energy is consumed; things wear down. Attention needs to be paid to infusing new resources, or refreshed resources, into the quest for improvement.

THE TENET OF TURNOVER

Turnover can damage school improvement work. If it happens at the leadership level, it can stop it dead in its tracks. The first message is obvious: Keep turnover in check. The second is less so: Make sure that everyone owns the improvement.

THE ADDITION FORMULA

Some of the school improvement literature sets changes up as dichotomies, with the resulting assumption that one or the other option is best. This is rarely the case. School improvement is almost always a matter of (cohesive) addition. For example, it isn't strong teacher leadership instead of strong principal leadership. It's both.

THE RULE OF MULTIPLE HANDS

It is wonderful to have a cluster of dedicated colleagues who are on point for an improvement effort. But if the school does not find a way to share the load with a significant percentage of the teachers, leaders will die off, the initiative will become marginalized, and/or improvement will flame out.

THE LAW OF REGRESSION

All the gravity in the school is going to try to pull reform back to the status quo ante, a type of regression to the norm. This tendency can be conquered, but only if it is understood and consciously addressed. Two steps forward and one back are fine. Two steps forward and five back are not.

THE TENET OF DOUBLE

Mark what you think can be accomplished in school improvement work. Double it. You and your colleagues will likely not reach this target. But you are apt to blow by the initial markers of success.

Source: Murphy (2011).

THE LAW OF REPLICATION

When given a blank sheet to work with, almost everyone will create the same picture of school improvement that he or she has drawn in the past. If you want or expect something different, new learning is in order.

Source: Murphy (2011).

THE IMPROVEMENT CODE

Almost everyone who writes or talks about improvement focuses on one dimension of the concept, the enhancement of results. But there is a second dimension that merits surfacing, the prevention of deterioration. This second aspect is often critically important for many schools at the beginning of reform efforts, especially those that are hemorrhaging failure.

THE STRUCTURAL TRAP

For many educators, school improvement is synonymous with the identification and importation of structural changes—block schedules, looping, detracking, academies, and so forth. This is problematic. An iron law of school improvement is that structural changes never have, do not now, and never will predict organizational success.

THE COMMON FAILURE

A good number of school improvement initiatives come to less-than-desired ends. No school wins all the time. And failure is never on vacation. This is normal. What is not routine is the planful employment of these results in the school improvement process. No one likes to poke at wounds. But schools are often too quick to haul their mistakes to the landfill, often tossing those blamed for failure on the trash heap as well. Schools committed to continuous improvement do not operate this way, however. They work hard to learn from missteps and failures. In so doing, they deepen cultural norms around risk taking and innovation.

Source: Murphy (2011).

THE REALITY OF THE CRUST

The core technology of schooling (instruction, curriculum, and assessment) is heavily buffered. What this means, of course, is that well-designed improvement efforts (e.g., policies, new programs) often bounce off the shell built up around learning and teaching or are used to harden the shell. You do not need to visit more than a few schools and a handful of classrooms to confirm that this is the case—and to affirm the frustration of everyone who strives to drive improvements into classrooms. Effective school improvement requires as much time devoted to peeling back this crust (e.g., fostering shared work) as it does to forging the change strategies.

THE RULE OF THE DENOMINATOR

School improvement has often been led astray by an infatuation with numerators. Individual numbers become decontextualized, assuming greater importance than they should. Those working on the school improvement work need to remember that it is their relationship to the denominator that provides importance to the numbers above the line.

Source: Murphy (2011).

THE ORDINANCE OF ABANDONMENT

For many schools, more is better. They continually add freight to an overloaded ship, often in an uncoordinated manner and almost inevitably without inquiring into what from the current manifest can be cut. The consequence is that people are overwhelmed more than they are helped. As Larry Lezotte and his colleagues made clear thirty years ago, school improvement work needs to attend to organized abandonment as well as to the hauling in of additional good ideas.

THE LAW OF CARVING STEW

Schools rarely mirror the tidy entities that most of us prefer. They are more like a stew than a meat and three meal. What does this tell us? First, different ingredients can work equally well. And they generally can be mixed in varying amounts and still produce a quite satisfactory outcome. Second, the almost maniacal need we have to chunk up the organization should be tempered somewhat. You cannot carve stew.

THE DOCTRINE OF THE FUTURE

Traveling backward rarely leads to the future. While revisiting keystone values is always desirable, perseverating over an unalterable past almost never is. Forensics in school improvement work can be quite valuable, but almost never when it is decoupled from strategizing the future.

Source: Murphy (2011).

THE PRINCIPLE OF PARSIMONY

In the world of school improvement, a handful of things done well is always better than a big bag of interventions.

THE PARADOX OF STRUCTURE

Earlier we reported that structures do not predict organizational outcomes. Here we add the second strand of structural DNA: In order to capture and employ reforms, good ideas need to assume form, that is, structure. The key to addressing the paradox is to ensure that form follows values and principles. Going in the opposite direction, that is, assuming the structure will alter values, is highly problematic.

THE LAW OF THE BACK DOOR

In school improvement work, it is easy to develop the habit of always trying to come in the front door. When our knock goes unrewarded, we pound louder. And then try to break the door down. Successful school improvement efforts teach us that there are almost always other ways to think about and address challenges. Doing the unsuccessful over and over out of stubbornness is not the same thing as persistence. Schools need to get in the habit of walking around challenges until they find a side or back door, doors that are often already open or at least unlocked.

Source: Murphy (2011).

THE CASE OF THE MISSING LINKAGES

School improvement activity often features a logic of action that is poorly coupled. N (e.g., shared governance) is coming to the school because it will lead to Z (e.g., better student learning outcomes). The problem is that there are a number of steps between N and Z. Linkages between these steps are often assumed to be operational but often are not. And when they are missing, movement toward improvement often grinds to a halt.

THE FALSEHOOD OF OZ

School improvement work is ongoing. The end point is always out in front. That is, as Mark Smylie reminds us, the term *continuous improvement* holds the high ground. School people who learn to be good at this work come to understand this reality. And they are effective in learning to appreciate the gains along the way. Those who do not are routinely disappointed that they never get to Oz.

THE RULE OF TIME

We know from colleagues such as Karen Seashore Louis that important changes take time. The improvement plant needs time to take root, to mature, and to flower. Those who keep pulling up one plant and replacing it with another will be disappointed. Exercise a little patience.

THE MARK OF COLLABORATION

Some school improvement work is derailed by an impoverished understanding of collaboration, by the acceptance of poor substitutes: Privileging the least robust points of agreement, dictated consensus, deferral to the hierarchy, and going along with the most aggressive of one's colleagues. Robust forms of collaboration power school improvement. Ersatz forms do not.

THE DOCTRINE OF TRUST

Earlier we reported that relationships power improvement. Here we add that trust powers relationships. A good deal of the enabling scaffolding for school improvement is about building webs of trust. And since it is inevitable in the rough-and-tumble of the work that threads will be cut, adding new threads must be an ongoing process.

THE PRINCIPLE OF THE FIRST FLOORS

There is a predilection in improvement work to look upward for wisdom. To be sure, those at the top are often good repositories of knowledge. But a considerable amount of wisdom can be garnered by those who are doing the heavy lifting on the ground floors, especially the teachers. The best school improvement work will capitalize on this truth.

THE DOCTRINE OF CONTEXT

Context is always important. The elements of school improvement are well known (e.g., quality instruction, personalized environment for students). But they need to be formed and polished to fit the specific context (e.g., level of school, type of clients).

THE CODE OF PERSISTENCE

Most school improvement work is hard; it isn't a smooth walk downhill. It is also almost a truism that people will get tired, grumpy, dispirited, and worse on the voyage—much of which is uphill and on crooked pathways. There will be points where it is clear to many if not most of the travelers that success is highly unlikely and that the trip should be suspended. It is important to push on at this point. Oftentimes the only thing that distinguishes successful from unsuccessful improvement efforts is persistence.

THE CONSEQUENCE PRINCIPLE

We know that there are consequences that rarely fuel continued improvement work. Many of these fall into the category of punishment (e.g., scapegoating, withdrawal of support). Others cluster in the domain of neglect. On the positive side of the ledger, we know that consequences around learning can power continuous improvement.

THE HEART OF SCHOOL IMPROVEMENT

School improvement is primarily about the development and inculcation of norms and values. These cultural elements need to be carried by the components of school improvement and set in place with structures, policies, systems, and practices. But it is the DNA that is being carried and set that is most critical.

THE BURNT BRIDGE PRINCIPLE

In school improvement work, there is a natural tendency to go backward. Schools need to be proactive to prevent this from happening. They have two options here. They can attempt to maintain constant vigilance over the roadway. Or they can burn bridges behind them so there is no easy way back. For example, if the school improvement design calls for an inquiry-based science program, make sure that the science textbooks are not still easily accessible.

THE FALSEHOOD OF THE SILVER BULLET

There is no silver bullet in school improvement. Nor is there a magic list. And no easy answers are lying about. What we know is that good school improvement designs identify and work on a handful of initiatives each of which adds a share to the overall gain. And they ensure that these initiatives are tightly linked.

THE CANNON OF PREVENTION

Moving uphill is almost always more difficult and more resource intensive than traveling on a flat road. In school improvement, this means that efforts to prevent problems always trump work to address problems once they appear.

THE LAW OF FRAGILITY

As Claude Goldenberg has helped us see, school improvement is fragile. It needs to be attended to with care. As the people engaged (e.g., early supporters, school leaders) begin to change or move on to new concerns and supports (e.g., social capital) are scaled back, there is a fairly good chance that the improvement initiative will fall apart—unless explicit attention is provided to these landscape-changing events.

THE RULE OF IN AND OUT

School improvement plans are most likely to be successful when they attend to conditions in the school (e.g., curriculum alignment) and factors outside the school (e.g., help available from social agencies).

THE TENDENCY OF CONTINUATION

One of the essential laws of social science is that past is prelude. The lessons for school improvement work are clear. The past needs to be disrupted, not massaged. And it would be wise to allocate work to those with a track record of success.

Source: Murphy (2011).

THE LAW OF THE SEEDBED

Improvement rarely occurs when the fact that there is a deep sediment of precedent in school is ignored. We have already highlighted the tough crust that has formed over learning and teaching. A good deal of sediment has also piled up in the domains of school organization and connections to the larger community around schooling. What we need to remember is that old seedbeds (e.g., transmission views of teaching, the hierarchical underpinnings of organizations) are toxic to many school improvement plants. Improvement initiatives do not change seedbeds; seedbeds change reforms. Much of the work of school improvement therefore needs to be about tearing up old seedbeds and creating new ones.

THE RULE OF THE ROADBLOCK

One of the most consistent findings in the area of school improvement is that things get in the way, and roadblocks are inevitable. When school people anticipate this and gather tools to tackle these barriers, improvement efforts can proceed. When they do not, they are often overwhelmed by the barriers and turn back.

THE PRINCIPLE OF NEUTRAL

Schools need to understand that there is no status quo when it comes to school improvement. There is no neutral. The school is either going forward or in reverse. When talk turns to maintaining ground already covered, it is likely that you are shifting into reverse.

Source: Murphy (2011).

THE LAW OF VARIABLE LIFTOFF

Scholars working to increase outcomes for students placed at risk need more of each effectiveness component to reach liftoff.

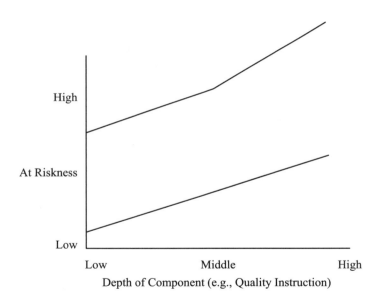

Depth of Component (e.g., Quality Instruction)

THE PRINCIPLE OF COHERENCE

Schools cannot improve when they are overloaded with disconnected change initiatives. They cannot reach their destination when teachers track in different directions. They cannot improve when the rules of the game are enforced in some places in the school but not others. And they cannot improve when goals, resources, and professional learning bear no relationship to each other. Consistency, alignment, integration, and coherence are at the heart of successful school improvement work.

THE DESIMONE LAW

Concrete, strong, and stable policies lead to stronger and deeper implementation, that is, more school improvement.

THE TENET OF EXISTING ASSETS

Most of us would like additional resources to do the work of school improvement. But improvement work often unfolds without new resources. Successful school improvement needs to be about using existing resources more productively and moving previously invested resources to where they are most needed.

THE RULE OF COMPRESSION

For school improvement to work, social and academic variability needs to be compressed. It is about high benchmarks for everyone and ensuring that each person conforms to those standards in every dimension of schooling—all day, every day.

THE DOCTRINE OF WINNING EARLY

School improvement goals are usually achieved in the far future. The distance between here and now and there and then can be quite lengthy. Change works best when it is chunked into manageable units so that ongoing victories are secured, especially in the early segments of the trip. Short term wins, as John Kotter has written about so thoughtfully, undermine skepticism and doubt and nurture the sense of possibility.

THE TEST OF SUCCESS

You will know that school improvement is working when people begin to believe in themselves and their work. More concretely, you can be assured that you are on the correct path when teachers begin to discover that their students can do all sorts of things that they thought were not possible.

THE RULE OF STRATEGICNESS

Throwing programs and initiatives one after another with the hope that something will work is an approach to school improvement that rarely bears fruit. Effective school improvement efforts are strategic. And strategy and its cousin coherence are generally seen together in improving schools.

THE ESSENTIALITY OF THE INFORMAL

We have nibbled at this idea already. The informal dynamics in schools exercise considerable influence over the success of improvement efforts. The key is to keep this reality at the forefront when planning for the work and during the work itself.

THE LAW OF MONITORING

When we look closely, we see that thoughtful monitoring is a critical element of school improvement. Only when there is a well-developed plan for checking that is followed with fidelity will improvement be possible. What gets monitored and fed back gets done. What doesn't does not.

THE NARRATIVE OF THE SINGLE WATERFALL

In a number of these lessons we have explained the importance of linkages in school improvement work, of cohesion and alignment. The absence of integration allows fragmentation to occupy the high ground. It ensures that a school will be run as a holding company. It significantly and negatively impacts improvement work. Another way to think about this is to envision effective school improvement as a single flow of water that cascades over all levels of the school district, from district, to school, to classroom—not as three separate waterfalls.

THE RULE OF DETAIL

The seemingly unimportant often ends up being important in school improvement work. Small things can derail change. School people need to get into the habit of examining and reexamining details.

THE MEANING OF SILENCE

Most of us fall into the bad habit of assuming that silence means agreement. No noise; no trouble. And then we are disappointed and shocked when labor is withheld at critical points in the work. An essential lesson from the school improvement literature is that silence does not equate with support. All people need to be brought into the discussion and heard.

THE TENET OF THREE ARMS

The nonnegotiable in school improvement is commitment to core values and principles. Strict adherence to a blueprint is not always needed or desirable. When all is said and done, an improvement effort with one leg and three arms is just fine if it includes the heart, soul, and mind you want.

CHANGE IS NOT IMPROVEMENT

One of the most critical errors that schools make is to equate change with improvement. The assumption is that things are better here because we have a new (fill in the blank). Things are better here because we changed the way (fill in the blank). Things are better here because we saw what (fill in the blank) was doing and we copied it. Change is the sine qua non of much improvement work. The problem is that there is not a strong connection between change and improvement. School people would do well to chisel this law on the keystone to the building.

THE TENET OF COMPLACENCY

As we have seen, if the process is managed well, much can be learned from failure. Success also needs to be managed. We know that success can breed more success. It can act as a catalyst for moving ahead. But it can also foster complacency, an unwillingness to move from ground gained through considerable hard work. The key is to learn to enjoy success but not to let the party run on too long.

THE PRINCIPLE OF THE BREAD CRUMBS

School improvement work done well can be exhilarating. It almost always has a strong future orientation. Way stations passed on the trip are often torn up to fuel the next stage of the voyage. But it is often useful to be able to follow progress backward to see where and why important travel decisions were made. The longer the improvement work goes on and the more the participants change, the more difficult the task will be if there is no record of the work. Be sure to leave a trail of bread crumbs so you can return to revisit key decisions.

THE 20% LOSS RULE

School improvement teams will never get 100% of what they want. So instead of saying that the school will get 100% of teachers to become active members of a learning community or 100% of their students engaged with a meaningful adult mentor, they shave 20% off the target and set the goal at 80%. What they forget is "the 20% loss rule." They will always lose 20% (or something of that magnitude). So when they set the target at 80%, they will still suffer the 20% loss, but they will end up with only 60% of what they want. If they set the goal at 100%, they are almost inevitably going to lose 20%. The difference is that they end up at 80%, not at 60%.

Source: Murphy (2011).

THE ORDINANCE OF HASTE

It is easy to work hard and not get anywhere. Driving fast around the beltway is not going to lead to school improvement.

ONE OF THE PRINCIPLES OF ALL

We have an undesirable habit in the school improvement world of shifting from one major category of interest to another, and with considerable force to boot. For example, we recently shifted to the "it's all about the kids" theme. It is difficult to take offense here. But there is a difference between arguing that kids are the core or that kids are first and saying that it is all about the kids. School improvement is about the teachers. And it is about the parents (customers) as well.

THE MULTIPLICATIVE LAW

We have described the importance of bringing a series of well-aligned strategies to school improvement work, of halting the search for the single solution. We noted the improvement gain is a composite of small increments. Here we also expose another lesson: The overall gain will be more than the sum of the individual increments.

THE ALLURE OF BUSYNESS

Busyness sometimes becomes an outcome in the school improvement equation, a measure of how good things are. There is no question that investment and hard work are important. But they are means to ends. In the world of school improvement, statements of investment always need to be linked to descriptions of bleeding that has been staunched and/or benefits that have been garnered.

THE PRINCIPLE OF DISCARD

It is not unusual for schools to mistakenly toss away good strategies in the struggle to get better. Most of this happens because insufficient time is allotted to see innovations come to fruition. But some discarding occurs because of a limited understanding of continuous improvement. Some important work is not going to carry people to the crest of the hill. But it can provide a strong platform for future work, a base camp that prevents free fall. Much initiative in the area of school culture, for example, is base-camp work. Do not discard haphazardly or prematurely, or without careful analysis.

Epilogue

The next and final time we see the three famous school improvement sleuths and their friend Mr. School Improvement, they have just completed facilitating a three-day workshop for leadership teams from all the middle schools in the Zolator Unified School District. They are seated at a table on the side of the multi-purpose room at the Archibald Middle School signing copies of their just-published book on the dos and don'ts of school improvement. Mr. Wolf looks up, catching the eye of an old friend at the back of the room. He offers his trademark grin, tips a cookie in that direction, and returns to signing copies of the book he wrote with his friends.

References

⊠   ⊠   ⊠

Bryk, A. S., Sebring, P. B., & Allensworth, E. (2010). *Organizing schools for improvement: Lessons from Chicago.* Chicago: University of Chicago Press.

Hattie, J. (2009). *Visible learning: A synthesis of over 800 meta-analyses relating to achievement.* New York: Routledge.

Murphy, J. (2011). *Essential lessons for leaders.* Thousand Oaks, CA: Corwin.

Index

Abandonment, ordinance of, 67
Addition formula, 57
Alignment, 93, 112
Allensworth, E., 29, 31
Allure of busyness, 113
Answers, decree of, 38

Back door, law of the, 72
Backward mapping, formula of, 36
Barriers to school improvement, 90
Block scheduling, 4
Boundaries, ordinance of, 52
Bread crumbs, principle of the, 108
Bryk, A. S., 29, 31
Building material of school improvement, 28–29, 29–30 (table)
Burnt bridge principle, 83
Busyness, allure of, 113

Cannon of prevention, 85
Carving stew, law of, 68
Case of the missing linkages, 73
Challenges, rule of, 37
Change is not improvement, 106
Closed eye, 51
Code of persistence, 80
Coherence, principle of, 93
Collaboration, mark of, 76
Commitment, law of, 50

Common failure, 64
Community sharing code, 41
Community support for school improvement, 22–23, 27, 41
Complacency, tenet of, 107
Compression, rule of, 96
Consequence principle, 81
Consistency, 93
Construction principles of school improvement, 30–32
Context, doctrine of, 79
Continuation, tendency of, 88
Continuous improvement, 74, 81
Crust, reality of the, 65

Deaf ear, principle of the, 51
Death of school improvement, 2–10
Decree of answers, 38
Denominator, rule of the, 66
Desimone law, 94
Detail, rule of, 103
Deterioration, prevention of, 62
Detracking plans, 4
Dip, law of the, 39
Disagreement, 46, 104
Discard, principle of, 114
Doctrine of context, 79
Doctrine of relationships, 49
Doctrine of the future, 69
Doctrine of the second eyeball, 42
Doctrine of trust, 77

Doctrine of winning early, 97
Double, tenet of, 60

Elmore, R., 50
Entropy, law of, 55
Equation, essential school
  improvement, 27, 28 (figure)
Equifinality, law of, 54
Essentiality of the informal, 100
Essential school improvement
  equation, 27, 28 (figure)
Existing assets, tenet of, 95

Failure, common, 64
Falsehood of Oz, 74
Falsehood of the silver
  bullet, 84
Focus of school improvement,
  10, 111
Formula of backward
  mapping, 36
Fragility, law of, 86
Fullan, M., 43
Future, doctrine of the, 69

Goals, long term, 97
Goldenberg, C., 86

Haste, ordinance of, 110
Hattie, J., 29
Heart of school improvement, 82
Hot house caution, 43

Improvement code, 62
In and out, rule of, 87
Informal, essentiality
  of the, 100
Inquiry programs, 4

Integration, 93, 102
Integrative dynamic, 31–32
Interim principals, 2

Kotter, J., 97

Law of carving stew, 68
Law of commitment, 50
Law of entropy, 55
Law of equifinality, 54
Law of fragility, 86
Law of monitoring, 101
Law of perceptions, 48
Law of regression, 59
Law of replication, 61
Law of the back door, 72
Law of the dip, 39
Law of the seedbed, 89
Law of the uninvited
  guest, 34
Law of variable lift off, 92
Lezotte, L., 67
Linkages, missing, 73, 102
Long term goals, 97

Mapping, formula of
  backward, 36
Mark of collaboration, 76
Martyr's creed, 53
Meaning of silence, 104
Missing linkages, 73, 102
Money and school improvement,
  6, 25
Monitoring, law of, 101
Multiple hands, rule of, 58
Multiplicative law, 112
Murphy, J., 35, 42, 46, 52, 60, 61,
  64, 66, 69, 72, 88, 91, 109

Narrative of the single
waterfall, 102
Neutral, principle of, 91

One of the principles
of all, 111
Ordinance of abandonment, 67
Ordinance of boundaries, 52
Ordinance of haste, 110
Organized abandonment, 67
Overpromising school
improvement, 13–17
Ownership of school
improvement, 56

Paradox of structure, 71
Parent advisory councils, 11
Parsimony, principles of, 70
Patience, 75
Perceptions, law of, 48
Persistence, code of, 80
Policies, concrete, strong, and
stable, 94
Power of up and down, 47
Prevention, cannon of, 85
Prevention of deterioration, 62
Principals, interim, 2
Principle of coherence, 93
Principle of discard, 114
Principle of neutral, 91
Principle of the bread
crumbs, 108
Principle of the deaf ear, 51
Principle of the first floors, 78
Principles of parsimony, 70
Principles of prolix, 40
Prolix, principles of, 40

Reality of the crust, 65
Reappearance of school
improvement, 11–18
Reculturing, 43
Regression, law of, 59
Relationships, doctrine of, 49
Replication, law of, 61
Resistance, 40
rule of, 44
Return of school improvement,
19–26
"Rightness," tendency of, 35
Roadblock, rule of the, 90
Rule of challenges, 37
Rule of compression, 96
Rule of detail, 103
Rule of in and out, 87
Rule of multiple hands, 58
Rule of resistance, 44
Rule of strategicness, 99
Rule of the denominator, 66
Rule of the roadblock, 90
Rule of time, 75

School improvement
alignment of, 93, 112
boundaries of, 52
broad picture in, 26
building material of, 28–29,
29–30 (table)
versus change, 106
commitment to, 50
community support for,
22–23, 27, 41
construction principles of,
30–32
context and, 79

as continuous, 74, 81
death of, 2–10
disagreement over, 46, 104
early wins, 97
essential equation, 27, 28
  (figure)
excessive reform packages
  and, 4
existing assets used in, 95
extended efforts at, 5
failed attempts at, 11–12,
  20–21, 72
fragility of, 86
fresh eyes in, 42
haste in, 110
heart of, 82
integration of, 93, 102
integrative dynamic, 31–32
keeping records of, 108
lack of focus in, 10, 111
lack of team effort in, 7–9, 58
magic fixes, 84
money and, 6, 25
monitoring of, 101
overpromising, 13–17
ownership of, 56
perceptions in, 48
persistence in, 80
preventing deterioration of, 62
reappearance of, 11–18
return of, 19–26
side effects of efforts at, 15
strategic, 99
structure and, 63, 71
success, 98, 107
supports, 30–31
time required for, 75
turnover and, 56

unintended consequences
  of, 34
Seashore Louis, K., 75
Sebring, P. B., 29, 31
Second eyeball, doctrine
  of the, 42
Seedbed, law of the, 89
Short term wins, 97
Silence, meaning of, 104
Silver bullet, falsehood of the, 84
Slope of improvement, 39
Smylie, M., 74
Social capital, 41
Socialization lapse, 45
Strategicness, rule of, 99
Structural trap, 63
Structure, paradox of, 71
Student advisory systems, 4
Success
  complacency and, 107
  test of, 98
Superintendents, 7, 12, 24
Supports, 30–31

Team effort in school
  improvement, 7–9, 58
Tendency of continuation, 88
Tendency of "rightness," 35
Tenet of complacency, 107
Tenet of double, 60
Tenet of existing assets, 95
Tenet of the three arms, 105
Tenet of turnover, 56
Tenet of up and down, 47
Test of success, 98
Three arms, tenet of the, 105
Time, rule of, 75
Trap, structural, 63

Trust, doctrine of, 77
Truth about disagreement, 46
Turnover, tenet of, 56
20% loss rule, 109

Uninvited guest, law of the, 34

Up and down, tenet of, 47

Variable lift off, law of, 92

Winning early, doctrine of, 97
Wisdom, 78

CORWIN

A SAGE Company

The Corwin logo—a raven striding across an open book—represents the union of courage and learning. Corwin is committed to improving education for all learners by publishing books and other professional development resources for those serving the field of PreK–12 education. By providing practical, hands-on materials, Corwin continues to carry out the promise of its motto: **"Helping Educators Do Their Work Better."**